TEXAS FARM & RANCH GUIDE

FOR BUYERS AND SELLERS OF TEXAS COUNTRY PROPERTY, RURAL LAND, AND ACREAGE

BRAD BEVERS

Texas Farm & Ranch Guide
For Buyers and Sellers of Texas Country Property, Rural Land and
Acreage

Published by Lucid Books in Brenham, TX.
www.LucidBooks.net

First Printing 2014

ISBN-10: 1935909991
ISBN-13: 978-1-935909-99-6

Special Sales: Most Lucid Books titles are available in special quantity
discounts. Custom imprinting or excerpting can also be done to fit special needs. Contact Lucid Books at info@lucidbooks.net.

About the Guide and Author

This **Texas Farm & Ranch Guide** was created to help buyers and sellers of country property in Texas meet their goals. I'd enjoy hearing from you if the guide is helpful to you in any way or if you would like to know more. I am an active farm and ranch real estate agent in Washington County. If you are looking to buy or sell in Texas, call or email today and I'll look forward to helping you achieve your real estate objectives.

www.TexasFarmAndRanchGuide.com

Brad Bevers, Broker Associate

brad@beversrealestate.com

936.443.6888

Bevers Real Estate

www.beversrealestate.com

7701 Highway 290 East

Chappell Hill, Texas 77426

979.830.1180

Contents

Introduction

B evers Real Estate is a farm and ranch real estate firm located in Chappell Hill, Texas. About an hour outside of Houston and an hour and a half from Austin, we have helped South Central Texans buy and sell real estate for over thirty years. Our clients include weekenders, ranchers, retirees, and families. We sell residential homes, empty lots, and businesses both large and small, but we are known for our expertise in farm and ranch real estate.

When my grandparents, Ken and Ann Bevers, looked at a map of Texas to decide where to start a real estate business, they chose Chappell Hill because of its beautiful landscape and the relatively short drive to several major metropolitan areas. They hoped that as the cities grew, so would their business. Time brought urban and rural development and expansion, and nearly a billion dollars worth of real estate has been bought and sold through Bevers Real Estate since they opened the doors in 1981.

The summer before I graduated from college my grandparents asked me to consider working with them in real estate. I was a senior at Texas A&M University and wasn't sure how I wanted to use my management degree. I took their advice and moved to Chappell Hill in 2004. Soon my Uncle Travis and Aunt Tracy joined as well, and we have had three generations working together ever since.

I believe a key to the success of Bevers Real Estate has been our focus on building relationships, not just closing a deal. Our partnerships extend far beyond any one transaction, and often span generations. Time and again I've had clients become friends, and what began as a job has turned into a profession I genuinely enjoy. It's my goal to help clients and friends buy and sell farm and ranch real estate with confidence. I created this guide to help others along the way.

The Bevers Real Estate agents I have worked with over the past ten years have been great colleagues from whom I have learned a lot. We are lucky to have had some of the best farm and ranch realtors working along with us. Two who stand out in particular are still with our company. Dave Wyatt teaches farm and ranch real estate courses across Texas to other realtors. Robert Lehmann is not only a good realtor, but a wildlife expert who is a valuable resource to our clients.

It has been a blessing to work with my grandparents and to know them professionally. They exhibit kindness, wisdom and integrity, and I have grown to appreciate working together with family over the past decade. In 2012, my Uncle Travis passed away suddenly and unexpectedly at fifty years of age. No one was better than Travis at dealing with the details of real estate in a gracious way with a quick smile. Travis, you inspired me to write this. Wish you were here to point out all the things I've missed.

Brad Bevers
January 2014

CHAPTER ONE

Choosing the Right Real Estate Agent

I f you have time to read just one chapter in this guide, read this one. Whether you are buying or selling, choosing the right professional to help you is the single most important thing you can do. While selecting the right agent is always important, it holds especially true in farm and ranch real estate. Here are two key suggestions to consider when choosing an agent:

1. *Find a farm and ranch agent with experience.* Any real estate agent can help you buy or sell a farm or ranch, but that doesn't mean he should. You need to choose an agent who is familiar with mineral rights, local agricultural resources, wildlife, tax exemptions, and other areas related to farm and ranch real estate. If you really like your residential realtor and want to give him a chance, remember that he will be learning on your dime.

2. *Build a long-term relationship.* Whether you are buying or selling, you will work with your farm and ranch realtor for much longer than your residential realtor. You need to choose someone who you enjoy and can really get along with, not just put up with for a short while. There will be less inventory to choose from and it will be located in a wider geographic area. The hunt for the right property can take months, or even years.

GETTING STARTED

These days, just about any search for a new home or property begins online. Log on to your local farm and ranch MLS (Multiple Listing Service – a group of listings that realtors have access to in a given area) and start your search. I recommend that you try:

> *www.TXLS.com* - Texas Listing Service, a great resource for finding farm and ranch property, especially in the South Central region of Texas.
>
> *www.LandsOfTexas.com* – A very good, statewide farm and ranch resource.
>
> *www.BeversRealEstate.com* - If you are interested in property between Houston and Austin, visit our website.

SELECTING A BUYERS AGENT

Narrow your options down to the three properties that best fit your criteria and call each of those agents. Ask some detailed questions about the properties, and note their responses. You are looking for a realtor who is knowledgeable about the listing, and you would like to have the confidence that he's speaking honestly. You should get a feel for who you would like to work with right away.

10 Questions to Ask When Contacting a Listing Agent

1. Can you tell me more about the mineral situation?
2. Are they conveying surface control?
3. Are there any encumbrances on the property?
4. How are the neighbors?
5. Is there a current survey?
6. Is it under an agricultural or wildlife exemption? How do they maintain it?
7. Are there any easements on the property?
8. Any current agricultural leases?
9. What's the average per-acre price in the area? How does this compare to the average and why?
10. What did your farm and ranch sales look like over the past twelve months?

This guide will go into more detail about what the answers to those questions might mean for you. I guarantee you that if you ask the agent these things you will come across as a knowledgeable farm and ranch buyer who is serious about a purchase.

One point to keep in mind: don't count it as a negative if they have to answer, "I don't know," every once in awhile. Farm and ranch real estate is a complex business, and if someone has all of the answers all the time then they are probably lying to you. If an agent says, "I don't know," they should offer to follow up and find out, and then actually do what they say. If they follow through, it's a good indicator that you are considering the right agent.

Select the agent you are the most impressed with and proceed from there. One agent can assist you with seeing each of the properties you're interested in, regardless of whether he is the listing agent or not.

AGENT LOYALTY

After you find an agent you enjoy working with, use him. Some clients worry that they are bothering their agent by calling too often and instead they contact the listing agent themselves to save their own agent time. Don't do that—your agent will be able to find more information for you faster, and it's his job.

Some companies won't work with another agent if a client contacts them first, so you may inadvertently cut your agent out of a deal. Call your agent until he asks you not to and, if that happens, it's time to find someone else anyways. Loyalty goes both ways in this business, and building a relationship that lasts will pay huge dividends for you down the road.

WARNING SIGNS

Sometimes a buyer can get started with a realtor who isn't looking out for the best interest of his clients. Here are some warning signs you should watch out for.

1. *Only promoting select listings.* If an agent is only showing you his own listings, then tread carefully. Agents that push the sale of one particular listing are usually more worried about making a sale than helping you find the right property.

2. *The used car salesman approach.* This goes along with the point above, but it's worth repeating. If an agent tries to push one particular listing or the first listing you see too hard, beware. Some agents forget that they aren't selling you a particular home or property. An agent should sell you on his own competence and expertise, not push any one property too hard.

3. *Dismissing negative issues.* If you notice a negative issue and bring it up, beware of an agent who dismisses the matter quickly. If there are easements, flood plain problems, or mineral issues, these are serious concerns that should be addressed appropriately. It may turn out to be minor, but your questions deserve honest, researched answers.

4. *Service contractor preferences.* You will need to rely on the expertise of your agent to provide you with lender recommendations, surveyors, inspectors, wildlife consultants, and much more. Beware of someone who only gives you one name to call unless they have a very good reason. If an agent does not have a recommendation for any given area, ask him why. It could be he hasn't been in the area long enough to give you the right level of service.

5. *Not listening to your preferences.* With farm and ranch real estate, time is at a premium. It may take you all day to see five properties, and you don't want to waste any time seeing land that you have already ruled out for one reason or another. Be clear about what you want.

SELECTING A LISTING AGENT

If you had to pick an agent based on one thing, what should it be? Years in the business? Current listings? Amiable personality? While these are valuable, there is one thing that stands out as the most critical.

The most important, single criteria to look for in an agent is a great internet presence.

According to the 2012 National Association of REALTORS® Profile of Home Buyers and Sellers, 90% of real estate buyers used the internet to gather information about the property. The internet is the single most used resource that buyers will find a property on, and it produces actionable results. 76% of buyers drove by a property after an internet search and 62% set an appointment to see it.

An internet presence indicates market savvy in an old business, and that matters even more in farm and ranch real estate for a few reasons:

- Most buyers find their property online. Farm and ranch buyers often buy in area that is an hour or more away from their full-time home, making an everyday, on-the-ground search less probable.

- Open houses don't work well for farm and ranch land, but great photographs and online listings do.

- Farm and ranch buyers often travel further to visit a property they're considering. A good online listing gives them a reason to make the trip.

All things being equal, choose the real estate agent with the best website. The site should have aerials, maps, multiple high quality pictures, detailed lists of property features, disclosures, and other information available online in multiple places.

10 Questions to Ask Your Potential Listing Agent

1. What are all of the websites where my property will be listed?
2. What is your company's website? Will it have maps, aerials, and disclosures posted? Who will take the pictures for the online property listing?
3. What information will you give buyers when they ask about our minerals?
4. What financing companies do you recommend to buyers for my type of property? Why?
5. Will you accompany showings? Why or why not?
6. Do you have the right equipment to show my property?
7. What should I do to get the property ready?
8. What comparables can you show me to support the valuation given?

9. If you represent the buyer and seller, what will your commission be? (Good question to ask no matter what the answer is. You want to see how they respond, because buyers will be asking them the same thing.)
10. Can you point me to recent references from satisfied clients?

CHAPTER TWO

The Perfect Property

When you are looking for farm and ranch property, take your time. Whether it's a recreational property or a full time move, it's an investment for the future as much as it is a property to enjoy.

Looking for land can be overwhelming because there are many options. In general, it's okay to be very firm on the property features you want to rule out, but try to stay open-minded within your price and size range. For instance, if you decide that you only want property between one and three acres with an existing pond five miles from Burton, you may be looking for a long time and miss out on some great options.

BEFORE YOU LOOK

When you are going to look at country property, you need to dress appropriately. You will hike through weeds and mud puddles, jump barb wire fences, and try to avoid other obstacles. Wear jeans, a long sleeve shirt if it's not too warm, and boots or an old pair of tennis shoes.

Here are some issues to consider when communicating your preferences to your agent:

Easements. Are you willing to look at a property that is accessed by an easement (a right to use the property of another without owning it)? Are you willing to look at property that has other easements through it, and if so, what kind? Roads, access to other land, rural power lines, high power lines, pipelines?

Mineral Rights. What are you looking for in regard to mineral rights? Just a surface waiver? 100% of the royalty rights? Partial royalty rights? Water and timber rights have become an issue in Texas as well. Make sure that all of the rights you want are still attached to the land.

Neighbors. Country property is mostly unrestricted. It's not unusual for large, meticulously maintained ranches to be next to smaller, less attractive properties. What kind of nearby properties will you rule out?

Water Features. Does the listing need to have an existing water feature such as a tank, pond, lake, live creek, seasonal creek, or spring?

Geographic Area. What counties or geographic area should your agent search?

Trees vs. Views. What is more important to you? Consider that you can always plant trees, but you can't plant a view.

Improvements. Does the property need to have any buildings on it? What about a barn, or a smaller home that can be utilized while you build?

The perfect property is hard to find, but if you know what you are looking for from the start you will have an easier time narrowing it down quickly. I have included a worksheet in Appendix A of this guide that you can fill out and give to your agent so that he knows what to look for. You can also find a copy at www.TexasFarmAndRanchGuide.com.

NEXT STEPS

After you find a property or two that meets all of your general criteria, congratulations! The next thing you will want to do is to investigate the listing to the best of your ability. Here is a list of what you should consider before purchasing any property.

Inspections

- **General Inspection**. If there is a home or any other improvements on the property, pay to have it inspected *no matter what*. Even if you are 90% sure the structure will be torn down, an inspection will help you determine if anything could be saved, can help you negotiate a lower price, and will serve as a great punch list for projects to work on once you purchase the property. The inspection will almost always cost you less than $500, and it will save you much more than that.

- **Termite Inspection**. Have all improvements inspected for termites.

- **Water Well Inspection**. If there is a water well on the property, have a well inspector assess it. They will ensure that the flow is adequate and that there are not any mechanical problems. Note that this is different from a water-quality test, though many well inspectors can do this too.

- **Water Quality Test**. You can buy a kit to test this yourself or have it professionally done. Most well inspectors can do this for an additional fee.

- **Septic Inspection**. There are many different kinds of septic systems, and a professional can make certain that the system has been maintained properly. Texas requires that aerobic systems be checked quarterly, and in that case you may just need to see the records.

- **Foundation Inspection**. If you have any concerns about the foundation, or if the general inspector recommends it, have a structural engineer inspect it. One word of warning—don't have a foundation company come out and assess it for you. They have a vested interest in telling you there are problems because that's the only way they will get paid. If you want an unbiased answer, hire a third party. It won't be money wasted because you can use the report to negotiate a lower price with a foundation company.

Warranties & Insurance

- **Home Warranty**. If there is a home on the property, buyers should ask the seller to pay for a home warranty. Sellers should always provide this as it is a very inexpensive way to help give the buyer peace of mind and protect the seller from any unforeseen issues. Buyers should be aware that the policy sellers pay for is typically a very basic warranty. You may want to upgrade it after closing to include a broader range of coverage.

- **Insurance**. Talk to your insurance company as soon as you can about the transaction and make sure they are comfortable insuring farm and ranch property. Many urban insurance companies aren't familiar with rural property and may have a problem with the improvements, lack of a local fire department, or other rural issues.

- **Other Insurance Issues**. When buying a farm or ranch, consider carrying a higher liability policy. I sold a game ranch that is located on a fairly busy highway, and they had two dozen elk on the property. After talking it over, they decided to carry extra insurance because if there was ever a breech in the fence, an elk on the highway is a real danger. Consider the purpose of the property you're purchasing and decide whether this might be a good idea.

- **Life Insurance**. Not something you usually think about when purchasing a property, but if you use a rural land lender they will often ask if you are interested in a life insurance policy that would pay off the property in the event of your death. Ask them before you get to the closing table for details if you are interested in this.

Neighborhood

- **Appearance**. The overall feel of the area where you buy property is very important. You should always ask yourself, and your agent, if the area around the property is expected to be more or less valuable in ten years.

- **Your Local Community**. Is there anything that you place a high value on that you want to make sure is located nearby? Examples include hospitals, horse facilities, good restaurants, antique stores, or grocery stores.

- **Neighboring Land Uses**. What do the neighbors do with their land? Things to look out for that will influence resale value include large cattle slaughtering operations, chicken farms, pig farms, manure dump sites, high power lines, oil and gas activity, and anything that could be considered an eyesore. Always walk or drive the boundaries of the property before purchasing. I once found the perfect weekend property for some clients looking for a forty-acre tract. We decided to walk the boundaries before making an offer and as we hiked through the woods we saw some swimmers in a giant swimming pool on the adjacent property. Turns out that next door there was a nudist retreat that the listing agent had neglected to mention.

- **Road Noise**. If you are purchasing a property in the country, you might not care about the road noise. After all, anything is quiet when compared to the city. However, you need to be aware of the current noise pollution on the subject property and evaluate if it is expected to increase or decrease in the coming years because it could impact your resale value. Also be aware of nearby railroads. Check a recent aerial map to be sure that you don't miss something.

- **Timing Is Everything**. You need to look at a property at different times of the day before making a purchase. Try to get an idea of what is going on in the morning, afternoon, and evening near your property. Another type of timing you want to be aware of is seasonal timing. This is harder to determine for yourself, but ask your agent about traffic increases due to local festivals, craft fairs, and other seasonal activities. These can often be positives and boost the value of your property, but it's good to be aware of them. Also, some properties that look dormant in the winter months could turn out to be dead in the spring. Be aware that as the seasons change, your property will as well.

Infrastructure

- **Access**. Is it easy to get to the property? You can have quick access and a shorter trip from your full-time home to a weekend property, or you can have privacy and seclusion. It's rare to have both.

- **Utilities**. Is the property on a water well or community water system? Does the property have electricity available on site already? If not, how far away is it? If the property does not have electricity on it, you need to make sure that one of the neighbors will allow an electric easement. If they don't, you might be stuck without electricity on your land or have to overpay to get it there. Does the property have a septic system, or is it on a sewer system? If it is a septic system, what kind is it, and when was it last inspected?

- **Technology Needs**. Internet access and cell phone service is essential to many buyers, and you need to know your options before purchasing the property. Rural areas often have spotty service.

- **Drainage**. Does the property drain properly? Are any portions of the property in the flood plain?

- **Other Services**. Does the property have mail service? What are the options for trash disposal?

Environmental Factors

- **Environmental Study**. When you purchase a farm and ranch property, you have the right to investigate the environmental aspects of the property further. There is an environmental addendum that your agent can add to the contract that will allow you to research how it will impact your use of the land.

- **Dumps and Other Contamination**. Another good reason to walk the property in its entirety is to look for any dump sites. It is not unusual to find large trash dumps on country properties, and it's helpful to at least take a look and make sure that you are comfortable with the type of trash disposed there and determine if and how it needs to be cleaned up.

Taxes

- **Exemptions**. You need to be aware of what exemptions are on the property and what has been done to maintain them. If there is an agricultural exemption on the property, knowing how it has been maintained in the past is key in planning for the future. WARNING: If you buy land and the agricultural exemption is removed, you could be responsible for five years of rollback taxes. Talk with your county taxing authority before the transaction to be sure this doesn't happen.

- **Tax Value**. While the value on the tax rolls rarely corresponds with the market value, it is still helpful to know. Knowing the value the property is assessed at currently will help determine how much property taxes will be raised after a purchase.

Boundaries

- **Survey**. If you are buying country property through a lender, you will need an accurate survey. The party that pays for the survey is negotiable and the cost can vary widely. In general, lenders prefer a survey that:

  - Is under ten years old.

  - Has no more than one previous owner.

  - Accurately depicts all current improvements.

- **Fencing**. Does the property have perimeter fencing all the way around the property? Cross-fencing? Is it easy to tell where the property boundaries are, or do you need a surveyor to come out and mark boundaries to be sure?

Community Factors

- **County Restrictions**. Find out what the property restrictions are in the county you are considering. Each county is different and you need to make sure you can use the property for your intended purpose.

- **Septic Requirements**. Many counties in Texas place specific requirements on septic systems. If you are going to be adding one, you should know whether or not they will require an aerobic system or if you are free to put in one of your choosing. Aerobic systems require more maintenance and inspections by law.

- **Zoning**. Is the property zoned for any specific purpose? Farm and ranch property is often not zoned at all, but it's worth checking.

- **Local Schools**. Whether you have children or not, be aware of the local schools and their reputation relative to other surrounding school districts. Even if you don't have children or are just using this as a weekend place, a school district's reputation can impact the target market for the property when you sell.

For an easy-to-use checklist of the criteria we've mentioned, see Appendix B. You can also find a copy at www.TexasFarmAndRanchGuide.com.

CHAPTER THREE

Valuing the Property

F arm and ranch property is harder to place an exact value on than property located in a more urban area. There is a variety of reasons for this, but none greater than the lack of comparable sales for similar properties.

Farm and ranch tracts are often so unique that it is hard to compare nearby sales with the subject property and come up with an exact value. For this reason, it is important to find an agent who is trustworthy and familiar with the area. A farm and ranch real estate agent can quickly give you a number for what he thinks a property is worth per acre because he has represented buyers who have purchased similar properties.

Even though it's not an exact science, there are a number of factors concerning value you should consider when buying a property. These include average land price nearby, the effect of negative features (flood plain, lack of minerals or surface control, etc.), and the desirability of the area. Similar to a city, areas and values can vary widely from one road to the next.

4 KEYS TO A GOOD REAL ESTATE INVESTMENT

There are four ways to make money on real estate: buying undervalued property, buying income-producing property, making capital improvements, and waiting for market appreciation.

Buying Undervalued Property

This is probably the easiest way to insure a good investment in real estate. There are usually properties on the market that are undervalued because they don't quite fit the current target market, are being marketed poorly, or have challenging features that need to be overcome. It may sound unlikely or even impossible, but you can buy a farm and ranch property, put very little into it, and sell the property for a significant profit in a short period. I have helped clients do exactly this a number of different times and, so far, they have always made a profit.

I was lucky enough to connect with a family from Houston when I first started in real estate that wanted to start investing in smaller tracts of land. These three women decided to look at the five least expensive pieces of land in the county and choose the one they thought had the most potential. Their plan was to clean it up and then put it back on the market at a higher price.

They added a culvert that made the property a little easier to drive and had the 15 acres shredded properly. In less than 18 months, they were able to sell the property for almost double what they paid for it and take home close to $100,000 profit.

Since then they have bought and sold five more properties. They have never lost money on a property and have always been able to flip within two years. The biggest expense has been a fence that they put in on one property, but other than that very little has been improved before reselling the property.

There are opportunities to do this with farm and ranch property, large or small, because of the significant gap between the lowest price per acre in the county and the highest price per acre. For example, you can buy land in Washington County for between $2,500 and $30,000 an acre. With the right agent, you can pick up a piece of land for a good price and then market it as a higher value piece of land once you have improved it.

Tips for searching for undervalued farm and ranch property:

- If you have limited funds, invest in a property without any residential improvements that could be taxed heavily and look for property that has an agricultural exemption. A tax exemption is often very easy to maintain and can lower the annual taxes on the property by 90% or more. Visit www.TexasFarmAndRanchGuide.com for more details.

- Look for a property that has an odd shape on paper. Potential buyers rule out many properties that look too narrow or too misshapen, but you can find some gems if you are willing to think outside the box. One type of property often undervalued is long, narrow tracts of land. They often look skinnier on paper than they do in person, and many buyers never go out to take a look.

- Alternatively, look for land with a lot of road frontage that could easily be split into smaller tracts that would bring a higher price per acre.

- Walk the land, all of it. You would not believe how many people purchase property without walking it. In fact, listing agents often neglect to do this as well. Walking a property will give you unexpected views, help you see features that others have missed, and give you a better feel for the land. You should also list with an agent who will walk the land and help convince buyers to walk it as well.

- Properties with challenges often offer a lot of value if you can find an easy way to overcome them. These include properties with multiple owners, flood plain property, property accessed by easement, properties that lack mineral rights, and even properties that have active mineral production on them.

The bottom line: when looking for undervalued property, go see the places that no one else is interested in. You will be surprised at what you find.

Buying Income-Producing Property

This is more difficult with farm and ranch property, but not impossible. Real estate investors often buy residential or commercial property for rental income, but farm and ranch property can be harder to monetize. Here are a few tips:

- If you live in a county with active mineral production, sometimes you will be able to get royalty income from minerals. This is becoming less and less likely as operators buy up mineral rights across Texas, but it is still possible to find land with the rights attached in certain areas.

- If there is a residence on the property, you can often rent it out if you don't plan to use it. This will most likely not pay the note on the property, but it will make a dent.

- Don't plan on making much, if anything, from leasing your property to farmers or hunters. The main advantage in doing this is the tax savings it will give you on an exemption, but it won't cover much more than that. For example, land often leases to cattle ranchers for grazing for $15-$20 an acre annually.

- If you have a large piece of land, you may be able to turn it into an income-producing hay operation. As gas prices continue to rise, local hay production will become more viable. In order to make this work, you will need a good irrigation system, a significant capital investment upfront, and at least a few hundred acres.

- It's also possible to create income-producing clubs that focus on farm and ranch activities (think hunting or horse-riding).

The bottom line: In order to find a farm and ranch property that produces significant income, you will have to think creatively and look for a variety of factors.

Improving the Property

Improving the property is the second best way to turn a farm and ranch property into a great investment. The goal is to make improvements that will bring a significantly higher return than their cost when you sell. For every dollar you put in, you want the property value to increase by two dollars.

Farm and ranch property gives you the opportunity to improve both the land and any structures, and you can often add a lot of value by doing so.

- If there is a home on the property, improve it if needed. You will get a larger bang for your buck here than with residential home improvement because a house that is valued at a higher price per square foot can also raise the per acre value of the land it sits on. If you are looking for areas to focus on, improve the kitchen, bathrooms, and landscaping.

- First impressions matter. Improving the road, driveway, and entrance to a property can make a big difference. Remember that by the time someone is entering a farm and ranch property they have probably already seen aerials, pictures, and disclosures. If you are able to exceed their expectations quickly, you will improve the perceived value of the entire property.

- For wooded property, create walking trails through the trees. This makes the property more usable and helps future buyers see more of it.

- Consider putting in a pond if the property does not have a water feature. Contact your local National Resources and Conservation Service (NRCS) office and they will help assess your land for a pond site at no cost to you. They may even help pay to put it in.

- Improve the fencing on the property. A property with a good fence in place will appeal to a wider market than one with a fence that is cobbled together.

- Highlight the best building site on vacant land. It may be a good investment to purchase a stand (like a high deer blind) to place at the best building site before you list so potential buyers can see the view from the building site.

- Improve the look of open fields. You can often have this done for free by leasing the land for hay production to a local farmer. They will fertilize it, water it, and plant grasses there. If the land is rough, you may need to pay for an initial root plow and weed eradication, but the property value will increase significantly if it goes from a weeded field to a rolling, grassy plain.

The bottom line: There are numerous capital improvements you can make to a farm and ranch property. Finding the right farm and ranch real estate agent to advise you on the highest value improvements for the area will pay huge dividends.

Market Appreciation

This is the last way to make money on a farm and ranch property, and the one that you have the least control over. There are a number of factors to consider when you are evaluating the potential appreciation of an area, and you need to be aware of the local, regional and state influences that will affect the property.

Local Factors

Be very aware of what road your property is located on and what other properties surround it. Is there a lot of oil and gas activity in the area? Are there similar size properties that could drive the value up, or are there smaller properties that could drive it down? How is this area relative to other areas surrounding it?

Remember that when you buy farm and ranch property you are buying unzoned, unrestricted property most of the time and your neighbors will as well. There are no guarantees about what will go in next door to you, so purchase a property that is less likely to be affected by neighboring properties.

Regional Factors

One of the largest drivers of value for farm and ranch property is regional growth and migration. If you buy a property that is located an hour outside of an urban area, it is likely that its value will increase more quickly than a property three hours outside of an urban area. As urban sprawl continues to expand in Texas, you will find many opportunities outside of more populated cities.

Texas

Texas is one of the best places to buy property right now. Reasons include the booming oil business, no state income tax, growing metropolitan areas, and the high employment rate. All of these factors help to keep the price of real estate in Texas headed in the right direction. Even before the recession ended in 2009, many areas of Texas never experienced a dip in property selling prices. Real estate did not appreciate, but owners did not lose much value either.

Relative to the other states, Texas is the best place to buy land in today's economic environment. The prices are stable, population is soaring, and the land is both beautiful and diverse.

The bottom line: If you are making the right first step by buying land in Texas, be sure and take the regional and local factors into account as well.

CHAPTER FOUR

The Farm and Ranch Contract

Most people don't purchase and sell farm and ranch properties every year. Because of the typically longer holding period, the standard contract may change significantly between your purchase and sale. It's best to have an experienced farm and ranch real estate agent represent you.

Currently, there are many unique features of the farm and ranch contract that you should pay attention to as either a buyer or seller.

ITEM 2.A: LEGAL DESCRIPTION

It's always important to pay close attention to the legal description, especially if the property you are purchasing hasn't been surveyed or does not have an address. In most of these cases you or your realtor should attach an exhibit to the offer that clearly shows what property you intend to purchase or sell.

ITEM 2.B: IMPROVEMENTS

Farm and ranch improvements are included by default in the standard farm and ranch contract provided by TREC (Texas Real Estate Commission). These are all "permanently installed and built-in items." Examples include windmills, tanks, barns, pens, fences, gates, sheds, outbuildings, and corrals.

ITEM 2.C: ACCESSORIES

Farm and ranch accessories must be marked or noted on the contract if you want them to stay. These are any items that are on the property, but not permanently installed or built-in. Accessories could include livestock feeders, irrigation equipment, hunting blinds, portable buildings, game feeders, and pressure tanks.

ITEM 2.D: CROPS

Seller has the right to harvest all of his crops until delivery of possession in the standard contract.

ITEM 2.F: RESERVATIONS

The mineral clause in a farm and ranch contract is very important to both buyers and sellers. Currently, the reservations clause reads as follows:

RESERVATIONS: Any reservation for oil, gas, or other minerals is described on the attached TREC addendum. Seller reserves the following water, timber, or other interests: _____

Note that if nothing is written here, and there is no TREC addendum attached addressing the minerals (TREC No. 44-1), then the seller is not reserving any of the minerals that he owns. Have your farm and ranch agent advise you on the mineral situation of the property, and be prepared to negotiate this point. Other than the price, the minerals are discussed more often than any other item on a rural contract. Remember that minerals are not guaranteed by the title company. You should always hire an experienced lawyer to assess the minerals that will convey with the property.

ITEM 6.C: SURVEY

Though not exclusive to a farm and ranch contract, the survey is very important and can be expensive. Pay close attention to what is agreed to here and remember that time is of the essence. There are specific timelines in the survey paragraph that must be adhered to closely. If you are a seller, be sure that you and your agent submit the T-47 document in the required time period.

ITEM 6.D: OBJECTIONS

Make sure that you give yourself enough time to make objections in this portion of the contract. Common objections would include mineral leases, surface leases, easement agreements, survey discrepancies, and flood plain. Once you object, the seller will have fifteen days to cure the objections or the contract may be terminated at the buyer's discretion.

ITEM 6.F: SURFACE LEASES

All leases, oral or written, must be disclosed by the seller. Unless noted on the contract, any leases that turn up after the contract is executed may be objected to under Paragraph 6.D. This is especially important on farm and ranch property because there are often grazing or hunting leases that you will want to be aware of.

ITEM 13.B: ROLLBACK TAXES

If you are buying a property that has an agricultural exemption, make sure that you know the requirements for keeping it in place. Conditions and enforcement can vary from county to county, so it's best to check with the local tax office beforehand or consult an experienced farm and ranch broker who is familiar with the area.

If the sale or a change in the use of the property results in an assessment of taxes or penalties, the buyer is responsible for paying them. This can be significant. When a property is taken out of an agricultural exemption, rollback taxes can be assessed as if the property was not exempt for the past five years.

• • • •

This is a quick overview of important points in the contract that you should pay close attention to as a buyer or seller. Of course, you should always read any real estate contract carefully before signing it and consult an experienced agent and a real estate lawyer as well.

CHAPTER FIVE

Let's Make a Deal

A fter finding the right agent and the perfect property, the only thing left is to make the deal. When you are considering making an offer on a farm and ranch property, all of the features and benefits should be taken into account. Have your agent come up with a fair, independent valuation based on comparable sales and make sure that you are comfortable with the value versus the price before moving forward.

MAKING THE OFFER

Don't be afraid to offer what you think is fair, even if it is pretty far off listing price. One way that farm and ranch property differs from residential property is that you will often be dealing with an investor, someone who inherited the land, or a weekend rancher. If someone is not using the property much, as opposed to a house where they live, they may be willing to come down off the price once they see an offer in front of them.

Of course, it goes both ways. Because many farm and ranch sales are want-to-sell properties and not have-to-sell properties, the seller may not be willing to budge. Again, having an independent evaluation and knowing what the property is worth will tell you if you are getting a great deal or not, even if they don't budge on price.

CHANGING YOUR MIND

There are a few ways that you are protected in a farm and ranch contract should you change your mind about the purchase.

Option Period: Just like for a home, you can build an option period into the contract. An option period gives the buyer a unilateral option to back out of the contract for any reason for a set period of time, and it is one of the most powerful tools buyers can use. They can lock up a property for very little and protect their earnest money while they evaluate the property. As a seller, you should limit the time on the option period to the minimum necessary amount for a buyer to evaluate property and make sure the option amount is fair.

Objections: When you purchase a larger piece of land, be prepared for a few surprises on the title commitment. The title commitment will disclose all of the exceptions to coverage and with a rural property, it can be staggering. I have closed some properties that have over 50 exceptions, from oil leases, mineral reservations, pipeline easements, grazing rights, and much more. If something comes up on the commitment or survey (or any other document for that matter), you will have a certain amount of time to object in writing. If the seller cannot cure the problem, the contract can be voided at the buyer's discretion. Consult an attorney on any of the objections that you would like removed or need clarification on.

Financing Addendum: As with any property, you can request a time period to seek the loan terms you want in order to have your earnest money protected. If the buyer is unable to find the terms they are seeking within the time period, they can exercise their right to get out of the contract.

AFTER THE SALE

Once you have completed the purchase of your property, it's time to make sure everything is in place before you relax.

Agricultural Exemption

If you have an agricultural exemption on the property, you should check with the county tax office as soon as possible. You will need to fill out a 1-D-1 form to keep the exemption in place when the time comes, and you want to talk to them and let them know you will be maintaining the exemption. Many tax offices are easy to work with, but make sure you get it right—if you lose the agricultural valuation you could be in for a very large tax bill.

Contractors

Make sure you have an agent who will keep working after the deal is closed. You will likely need a reliable set of contractors sooner than you think. This is especially true during hunting season in the country, when it can be very hard to even get a returned phone call.

Neighbors

Be sure and go meet your neighbors. On a large farm or ranch, it always helps when your neighbors know who owns the property and who should not be there. Neighbors can also help keep you informed about the community and area developments.

FINALLY . . .

Congratulations on the purchase of your farm and ranch property. Whether you've bought your property for recreational or professional use, owning land in the heart of Texas is something to be proud of. A lot of hard work goes into finding and purchasing the perfect property, and once you find the right place, enjoy it!

Be sure and visit www.TexasFarmAndRanchGuide.com for more helpful tips on buying property.

Appendix A

Property Search Criteria

Name: _____

Phone: _____

E-mail: _____

Mailing Address: _____

_____

_____

Location (counties or geographic locations desired): _____

_____

Desired Mineral Rights: ☐ Full   ☐ Partial   ☐ Surface

Water Features: ☐ Any   ☐ Pond   ☐ Live Creek
                        ☐ Seasonal Creek

Trees: ☐ Wooded   ☐ Mostly Cleared

Improvements: ☐ Raw Land Only ☐ Some Improvements
                        ☐ Move-In Ready

Access: ☐ Road Frontage Only   ☐ Easement Access Is Fine

Describe Desired Property Features: _____

_____

_____

Timeline To Purchase: ☐ Ready Right Now   ☐ 3-6 Months

☐ Within A Year   ☐ Unknown

Budget to stay under when searching: _____

Appendix B

Property Evaluation Checklist

Inspections

☐ General Inspection ordered & completed

☐ Termite inspection ordered & completed

☐ Water well inspection (if needed)

☐ Water quality test (if needed)

☐ Septic inspection (if needed)

☐ Foundation inspection completed (if needed)

Warranties & Insurance

☐ Home warranty ordered

☐ Insurance in place before closing

☐ Other insurance issues considered

Neighborhood

☐ Appearance—Satisfied with overall neighborhood and street?

☐ Your local community. Are desired services like hospitals, horse facilities, good restaurants, antiquing, and even grocery stores located nearby?

☐ Neighboring land uses are desirable.

☐ Noise pollution acceptable?

☐ Is property desirable at different times of day?

☐ Is property desirable during different seasons of the year?

Infrastructure

☐ **Access**. Is it easy to get to the property?

☐ Electric

☐ Water

☐ Septic/Sewer

☐ High Speed Internet

☐ Cell Service

☐ Mail Service

☐ Trash Service

Environmental Factors

☐ **Flood Plain**. Are any portions of the property in the flood plain?

☐ **Environmental study**. If desired, order this.

☐ **Dumps and other contamination**. Property searched?

Taxes

☐ **Tax Exemption**. Have you confirmed with county appraiser that property is currently under agricultural evaluation and will remain that way?

Boundaries

☐ Survey approved by all parties

☐ Fencing in good condition?

Community Factors

☐ Desired land use work with county restrictions?

☐ Septic Requirements in county determined?

☐ Zoning issues resolved?

Notes:

_____

_____

_____

_____

_____

_____

_____

_____

_____

_____

_____

_____

_____

_____

_____

_____

_____

_____

_____

www.ingramcontent.com/pod-product-compliance
Lightning Source LLC
Chambersburg PA
CBHW021338290326
41933CB00038B/962